Taking a walk through Rīga in the Art Nouveau era

ART NOUVEAU IN RĪGA

By Silvija Grosa

JUMAVA

UDK 72 (474.3 – 25) (084)
Gr 721

Consultant *Rihards Pētersons*

Translator *Kārlis Streips*

Designer *Arnis Rožkalns*

Editor of English *Iveta Boiko*

A map by Publishing House "Jāņa sēta" is used
for the design of the book

Photographers   *Vilnis Auziņš*
Leons Balodis
Ilgvars Gradovskis
Juris Kalniņš
Ainars Meiers
Imants Prēdelis
Indriķis Stūrmanis

Photographic materials of the Museum of Writing, Theater and Music,
the Riga Museum of History and Shipping, the State Museum of Art
are used in the book

Front cover — Alberta Street 13 (detail of the facade)
3rd p. — Elizabetes Street 33 (detail of the facade)

ISBN 9984–05–601–5

INTRODUCTION

The architecture of Rīga has changed many times over the course of the centuries, and the city now reflects these changes. Only a few periods in the development of Rīga, however, left as convincing the evidence as the late 19th and early 20th centuries — the period when Art Nouveau arrived in the city. The term "Art Nouveau" is used most often to describe the building arts in Rīga during that particular period of time. The architecture of the era was not stylistically homogeneous, but Art Nouveau unquestionably played a distinct role in the city's development: it pushed aside deeply rooted stereotypes, giving free rein to individualized freedom of expression. Art Nouveau, we must remember, appeared in order to cultivate aestheticized individualism, marking a counter-reaction to Historicism (Eclecticism), which prevailed in the 19th century. The ideal environment for an individual was seen as a detached single-family home, although in practice the style was most often used in the construction of large apartment buildings. This was one of the contradictory specifics of Art Nouveau, which is seen most vividly in the architecture of Rīga. The process of individualization was seen in apartment blocs by virtue of original designs and ideas. In the early 20th century, many Art Nouveau facades, including those in Rīga, bore the legend *Mans nams — mana pils* ("My Home is My Castle").

Just like in other parts of the world, exhibitions played an important role in Art Nouveau construction in Rīga, including the industrial and trade fair that was held in 1901 to commemorate the city's 700th anniversary. Also of importance were many periodicals which provided a look at other Art Nouveau centers in the world. These influences, however, cannot be seen more than impulses which facilitated a flourishing of Rigensian architecture and which were important in determining the specifics of the process.

In the late 19th and early 20th century, Rīga was one of the largest cities in the Russian Empire. It was an important regional center for economic and cultural life — a large city in the periphery of the empire in which economic and cultural life represented a mixture of German, Russian and Latvian interests. Rīga grew quickly, continuing changes which began in the latter half of the 19th century. According to the statistics of the time, between 1897 and 1913, the population of Rīga grew by 88%, reaching 530,000 people in 1914 which made Rīga the fifth largest city in the Russian Empire and the third largest (after St. Petersburg, which had 2.2 million residents, and Warsaw, with 884,000 people) in the Baltic region. For comparison's sake, we can look at Stockholm (350,000 residents), Helsinki (a population of 151,000) and Tallinn (140,000 people).

In the mid-19th century, when fortifications around Old Rīga were torn down and the city center was no longer reminiscent of a Medieval fortress, prohibitions against stone buildings outside of the city walls were lifted. This created proper conditions for the modernization of building traditions, and apartment buildings began to pop up in great numbers. The economic growth of the city allowed builders to achieve a great deal. Public buildings such as theaters, museums, hospitals and schools were erected, and much was done to improve the city's appearance. Sewage and water systems were

The Iron Bridge. Early 20th century postcard

improved, parks were installed, and bridges and viaducts were built. In the early 20th century, Rīga's streets were systematically widened, and the quality of street cover, according to specialists, was the best in the entire Russian Empire. Streets in the city center were lit with gas, while petroleum lamps were used in peripheral areas. There were several private electric power plants in Rīga in the early 20th century, and the city's own electrical central went on line in 1905 in the neighborhood of Andrejsala.

Since 1901 public transportation in Rīga was provided by electric trams. By 1905 there were already eight tram lines. The first automobiles appeared in the city in 1907, and three-seat uncovered taxicabs were first run by the Feitelbergs enterprising company in the same year. These taxicabs ran on three wheels and had a capacity of 3.5 horsepower. Cars could not yet compete with horse-drawn carriages, however. In 1910, there were 88 cars and 22 motorcycles in the Vidzeme Administrative District of which Rīga was part, while in 1913 there were still more than 1,000 larger and smaller horse-drawn wagons for public use.

The establishment of a ring of boulevards around the Old City was completed by the end of the 19th century, and most building work involved wooden structures in suburban areas that had emerged in the mid-19th century when Rīga was greatly influenced by industrialization, and rural residents flowed into the city. By the 1890s, however, stone buildings were common throughout the area outside of the former city walls.

Wooden buildings were often torn down and replaced by multy-story stone buildings. What is now the Central District of Rīga was the scene for particularly active construction work. The district is delimited by the ring of boulevards on one end and the city's railway system on the other. In 1904, new

building regulations were adopted which prohibited the building of wooden structures in the city center and "wooden Rīga" gradually capitulated before "stone Rīga". Today only a few wooden buildings have survived in the city center. The majority of wooden constructions is concentrated in Pārdaugava, Grīziņkalns and other suburbs of Rīga, forming unique, yet often untended "islands".

At the basis of the city construction of Rīga there is a regular network of streets where uniformity of construction is achieved by division of the land into plots. Each plot was built up on the basis of the principle of perimeter construction, although in some cases so-called half-open construction was used.

In the late 19th and early 20th century, public buildings and single family homes were erected, but most of the focus was on multi-story apartment buildings with space for stores and offices on the ground floor in many instances. The owners of these buildings were enterprising people of various ethnic groups, among whom the first Latvians appeared in the late 19th century. Obviously, apartment buildings were put up for reasons of profit, so stone Rīga is densely built up. There were strict building regulations, however, which limited the height of buildings in relation to the width of the street, about the placement of buildings vis-a-vis the "red line" of the street, etc. Architects and builders were highly professional, and all of the buildings from this period were of a very high quality. Buildings were put up quickly — in one or no more than a few years. Most of the work was done during the spring and summer. Once a design was approved, the foundations were laid and brickwork was done. Stone was allowed to "rest" during the winter, and final work was done the next spring. When the building was completed, a special commission issued an authorization for its use.

Brivibas Boulevard. Early 20th century postcard

The style of the new buildings reflected the way in which European architecture was developing at the time. Historicism underwent a crisis also in Rīga in the late 19th century, and architects began to look for new ways of approaching the building arts. Art Nouveau proposed radically new architectural principles. Buildings were put up on the basis of functional logic, and architects did not avoid asymmetrical approaches nor did they make efforts to subject the construction of the facade to an evenly rhythmic structure. Though the rational nucleus of a building was emphasized and interiors were subjected to functional logic, Art Nouveau also focused very much on aesthetic qualities. These are two fields of activity which cannot be separated. Art Nouveau placed great emphasis on decorations and ornaments, where the formal techniques of the new style — asymmetry and stress on the line — were brilliantly expressed. Popularity of decorations reflected the Neo-Romantic mood of the era where the obvious intention was to depict universal beauty. The ornamental aspects of older styles of art were not rejected, but they were changed and expanded to include new subjects, — Art Nouveau, we can say, had a specific iconography. Of importance were links between Art Nouveau and Symbolism, therefore decorations usually involved specific symbolic content.

In Rīga's architecture, Art Nouveau was used in parallel to certain elements of Historicism for quite some time, because the city's official circles were fairly reserved when it came to the language of form which the new style offered. The exterior of public buildings in the early 20th century more often used the principles of Historism, yet rejection of unification can be attributed to the influence of Art Nouveau.

In the early period of Art Nouveau architecture in Rīga (1898–1905), influences from several major Art Nouveau centers, especially in Germany, were of key importance. Rational and modern planning could often be merged with stylized motifs from historical styles in the facades of buildings. In other cases quite an opposite tendency could be observed when Art Nouveau ornamentation was used in buildings which were basically done in the style of Historism. Toward the end of the period, by the two principles having flown together, an increasing consistency in understanding Art Nouveau started to dominate. The decorative motifs that were used in Art Nouveau decorations — all manner of flora and fauna, and fantastic creatures — came from the field of "Biological Romanticism". Linked to the various areas of Symbolism, these ornaments pointed to the changing nature of the natural world and its internal strength. The decorative motifs became an object of aesthetics, leading to their rich use both in facades and interiors of Art Nouveau buildings of Rīga.

Raiņa Boulevard. Early 20th century postcard

Among the many masters of Art Nouveau architecture in Rīga, prominent individuals included Alfred Aschenkampf, Heinrich Scheel, Friedrich Scheffel, Konstantīns Pēkšēns, Mikhail Eisenstein, Wilhelm Neumann, Wilhelm Bockslaff, Paul Mandelstamm, Augusts Reinbergs, Jānis Alksnis, etc.

Around 1905 and 1906, the development of Art Nouveau in Rīga went off in two directions. The appearance of Art Nouveau facades and interiors changed significantly between 1906 and 1914, mostly under the influence of styles in Europe, and especially in Finland. Also of importance were the dramatic events of 1905 in Latvia, that made people look at many phenomena from quite a different angle.

During the later period of Art Nouveau, interest in the functions of the spatial structures of a building began to appear. The structure of the decoration on facades also changed. Asymmetric principles and emphasized lines were particularly clear in the use of

The Daugava Embankment. Early 20th century postcard

Vērmanes Garden. Early 20th century postcard

engraved ornaments, where linear drawings were sometimes supplemented with lightly plastic models. More reticent but varied decorative motifs were interpreted with delicate elegance, that testifies to excellent mastery of the principles of Art Nouveau construction. Ornamental decor was no longer used to subordinate the building, and powerfully accented and naturalistic ornaments were replaced by decor with a higher level of stylization. In the late period, much greater importance in facade decorations was given to the materials, as well as to the architectonic elements that were put to use; there appeared a tendency to accentuate vertical elements of buildings (so-called Perpendicular Art Nouveau).

Important changes were also related to National Romanticism, which arrived in Rīga's architecture in 1905/1906. The decorative forms of National Romanticism were quite geometric, which suggests that the style may have been a counter-reaction to early Art Nouveau, but in fact it was a modification of Art Nouveau. National Romanticism in Rīga was a phenomenon which focused (albeit not exclusively) on a search for a national style. The use of natural materials, their combinations and the dominance of hard corners in designs were of key importance. Facades were finished with rough and uneven stone, and the texture often used elements from Latvian folklore, stylized motifs of local flora and fauna, though traditional Art Nouveau elements were also put to use.

In the early 20th century, Latvia, like much of Europe, was a place where architects were eagerly looking for a national style, but we cannot say with certainty that National Romanticism was universally accepted as the best way to bring these ideas to life. Theoretical viewpoints expressed by participants of the process at the time suggest that issues were not always handled with clear answers. In a situation where early Art Nouveau appeared to have exhausted itself, while new solutions were not yet sufficiently convincing, the decorative appearance of buildings often harkened back to classical styles which could be merged with National Romanticism. Thus facades and interiors, beginning in 1906, started to display elements of Neo-Classicism which, however, was not an orthodox style in Rīga. Neo-Classicism could as well be combined together with elements of Art Nouveau and National Romanticism.

A number of prominent architects from the older generation continued working in the period of late Art Nouveau, but an important role was played also by a younger generation of architects, including Eižens Laube, Aleksandrs Vanags, Augusts Malvess, Eižens Pole, Edgar Friesendorff and others. The importance of the Faculty of Architecture at the Rīga Polytechnic Institute was key in establishing the city's architectural style. The young architects were innovators,

Society "Ziemeļblāzma". Early 20th century postcard

Elizabetes Street. Early 20th century postcard

searching for new forms of expression which clearly outlined the contours of the coming era.

Architects, of course, are responsible for the construction of a building, however much importance in its outer appearance belongs also to masters of decoration, and it is always interesting to identify them when looking at a building. Most of these people were foreigners who came to Rīga to earn money. Advertisements and information from address books show that between 1900 and 1905 there were around 20 working sculptors in Rīga. The largest building sculpture company in Rīga around 1900 belonged to August Volz. Other companies which enjoyed greater or lesser success included "Otto & Wassil", "Lotze & Stoll" and others.

Interiors during the Art Nouveau period involved the principle of ensemble-based solutions, and of importance were stained glass windows, ceramic tile panels, majolica stoves and decorative paintings. These jobs were done by local companies, although products that were imported from other parts of the world were also important. It has to be noted that several companies performed regular orders outside of Latvia. August Volz, for example, handled major projects in Tallinn, while the Ernst Tode stained glass workshop regularly received commissions from St. Petersburg and other cities.

We have good reason to be proud of the many Art Nouveau buildings in Rīga, among them true masterpieces of the style. Before we begin our tour of Rīga, we should remember the process of change which affected the buildings of the late 19th and early 20th century. Today we can feel very different emotions about these structures. We can enjoy those that are still intact, but we can also feel sorrow about those that have been lost altogether, as well as those in which "little details" such as window frames, stained glass windows and ceramic tile panels have been destroyed or damaged. Still, the possibility to observe a number of buildings and interiors restored over the last several years, allows one to better feel the charm of the Art Nouveau era.

Designer
Heinrich Siecke.
Stained glass windows

Audēju Street 7

OLD RĪGA

*Audēju Street–Peitavas Street–Alksnāja Street–
Kalēju Street–Teātra Street–Vaļņu Street–Kaļķu Street–
Šķūņu Street–Jauniela–Dome Square–Jēkaba Street–
Smilšu Street*

The story of Art Nouveau in Rīga begins in the city's oldest part — Old Rīga, where an ancient Livonian settlement was located more than 1,000 years ago. In 1201, Bishop Albert ordered the building of a residence for himself along with fortifications. This launched the Medieval period in Rīga, elements of which can still be felt today. As the time passed by, the rather limited territory, until the 19th century encircled by fortification walls, witnessed active construction. Building regulations of Rīga which dictated the maximum height of structures and great respect for the architecture of previous eras preserved its significance up to the late 19th century, when Art Nouveau arrived.

The first evidence of Art Nouveau can be seen in the apartment and shop building at **Audēju Street 7** (architect Alfred Aschenkampf: construction works begun in 1899) that belonged to the well-known publisher Alexander Grosset. The decorations on the fa-

Audēju Street 9. Detail of the facade

cade include the plant-based motifs that were so popular in Art Nouveau — irises, blossoming trees and reedmace —, as well as mascarons, which testify to the world of fantastic images. The building is a good example of the way in which the range of ornamental motifs was expanded in pursuit of Art Nouveau's "Biological Romanticism". Art Nouveau did not arrive in Rīga as a contradiction to Historicism. Rather, it grew out of the older style, and the flowing together of stylistic elements, even within a single building, can best be seen in structures that were put up around 1900.

The co-existence of Historicism and At Nouveau can also be seen in the apartment building at **Audēju Street 9** (1900, architect Konstantīns Pēkšēns). The motif of the sun in the pediment represents new life prosperity and its variations are found in numerous facades in Rīga.

A notion about the way in which the style developed in Rīga can be obtained when looking at the

Grēcinieku Street 2

synagogue in Peitavas Street 1, designed by architect Wilhelm Neumann in 1903. This was one of the earliest examples of an interaction between Art Nouveau and more classical elements in style.

Toward the Daugava River we find a number of buildings whose facades reflect the developmental processes which influenced Rīga's architecture alongside rationalist tendencies that appeared after 1905.

The apartment and shop building at **Grēcinieku Street 2** (1911, architect Paul Mandelstamm) is a good example of this. In the building at Grēcinieku Street 4, where an Irish pub is located today, the romantic Reimer's cafe was found in the early 20th century.

If we look at the facades in Kalēju Street, we can study several of the decorative techniques and motifs

Kalēju Street 41. Detail of the facade

that were popular in Rīga's architecture. The apartment buildings at **Kalēju Street 41** (1907, architect Rudolf Philipp Dohnberg) and **Kalēju Street 43** (1897, engineer Florian von Wyganovski) are decorated with dragon motifs — one of the most popular elements in architectural decorations at the turn of the century that testifies to the close links between Art Nouveau and Symbolism. The iconography of the dragon motif is wide and complicated. According to one of interpretations the dragon protected one's property and represented great wealth. The building at No. 43 belonged to advertising company owner Arthur von Grothus who published some of Rīga's first address books — a very important reference source at that time. The building and its decorations are typical of late Historicism. Similar to this is also the building at

Kalēju Street 43. Detail of the facade

Kalēju Street 49

Kalēju Street 49 (1901, architect Wilhelm Bockslaff) with rhythmically arranged "demonic" mascarons on the facade that was typical of the late period of Historicism. The motif is lacking individual uniqueness, however, and that is probably why the decorations on the building are supplemented with the shape of mythical Mercury on the pediment and two roosters in the relief above the portal (the rooster was one of Mercury's symbolic attributes). The image of Mercury as well as the rod-caduceus (the symbol of successful trade) — are frequent elements in decorations of Rīga's buildings and became especially popular in the period of late Art Nouveau.

The apartment and shop building at **Kalēju**

Kalēju Street 23

Kalēju Street 23.
Detail of the facade

Kalēju Street 6. Detail of the facade

Street 23 (1903, architect Paul Mandelstamm) attracts our attention with the lovely corner portal which is shaped like a leafy tree.

The turn-of-the-century building at Kalēju Street 18/20 houses the city's main pawn shop, and the facade is interesting because of the contrast between red brick and the texture of the plastered surfaces.

The facades of the apartment building at Kalēju Street 14/16 are decorated with purposefully retrospective techniques, which suggest of a great respect for the Medieval urban environment and involve reliefs with putti, caducei and others that were typical of late Art Nouveau, including also design elements which point to the occupation of the building's owner. These are techniques which are typically seen in the decor of other buildings in Rīga, too.

The small apartment and shop building at **Kalēju Street 6** has a facade which is decorated quite humbly — rectangular forms with floral motifs, as well as carved ornaments that were typical of late Art Nou-

Teātra Street 9. Atlases with the globe

veau. One can still see an impressive metal work on the facade — a flag holder in the form of a stylized dragon. The original window frames on the upper floors make the building live and attractive.

We must cross Riharda Vāgnera Street in order to find the building that is at **Teātra Street 9**. I would like to note that during the era of Art Nouveau, music had a priority in the inter-hierarchical system of various forms of art. The music and theoretical works of Richard Wagner was of key significance, and the great composer, who lived in Rīga from 1837 until 1839, is commemorated both in the name of the street and the music hall, which is located at Riharda Vāgnera Street 4.

The majestic and atectonic building at Teātra Street 9 (1903, architects Heinrich Scheel, Friedrich Scheffel, decorative sculptures by "Wassil & Co.") is

Teātra Street 9

one of the turn-of-the-century buildings in which we see elements of the Baroque, as well as of Art Nouveau.

The building was owned by C.J.Sichmann — trader of books and antiques. Perhaps that is why the building's appearance is somewhat reminiscent of antiquity with the images of Athena and Hermeus in a corner relief. The figures of Atlas that are at the top of the building were produced in the workshop of the sculptor August Volz. The globe, which is made of glass and zinc, was lit up at night, and it could be seen as a demonstration of the new technologies of the day.

Meistaru Street 10

As we walk along Vaļņu Street in the direction of Kaļķu Street, it behooves us to remember that the site at Vaļņu Street 20 once was occupied by the pastorate of St. Peter's Church. The structure was designed by Henry van de Velde and was destroyed during World War II. The building was put up around 1910, and the distinguished Belgian master of Art Nouveau occasionally visited Rīga to oversee the work.

Kaļķu Street divides Old Rīga into two parts. At one edge of Līvu Square, there is a very typical turn-of-the-century apartment and shop building, at **Meistaru Street 10** (1909, architect Friedrich Scheffel). One look at the little towers will tell you why it is popularly known as the "Cat building". The structure has an expressive silhouette and plastically softened forms of the facade. One of the portals has an Art Nouveau mascaron, while the other one has a figural relief that tells a realistic story. Similar decorations were found on many buildings constructed between 1907 and 1914, and usually the reliefs had something to say about the aesthetic ideals of the owners of the buildings. Story-telling on reliefs does not always allow us to know exactly what was meant by the artwork, however the representation of labor, for example, usually reaches the aim by fairly didactic intonation in expressing the importance of hard work in a human being's life.

Kaļķu Street 15

One of the earliest bank buildings in the area is the former Vidzeme Mutual Credit Society Bank at Kaļķu Street 11 (1902, architect Konstantīns Pēkšēns). The facade of the building has very clear representations of wealth "encoded" in emblematic reliefs. However, this is an exception — most bank buildings in Rīga used more universal and easily interpreted techniques, especially from the vast arsenal of Neo-Classicism. A characteristic example in this respect is the building at the corner of Kaļķu and Vaļņu streets (**Kaļķu Street 15**, 1913, architect Jānis Alksnis, the construction company "L. Schneider") that was occupied by the Rīga Pārdaugava Mutual Credit Society

Bank and other companies. Being a typical Neo-Classicist building from the early 20th century, its appearance definitely reflects the representative function of the bank. The building is important in the history of Rīga's architecture by being one of the first constructions to have a monolith ferro-concrete carcass.

The influence of Neo-Classicism can also be seen in a number of other buildings in the area. There is Balkin's building at Kaļķu Street 24 (1913–1917, architect H. Tiemer), which housed stores, offices and a cinema, also Tāls' building of shops and offices at Kaļķu Street 22 (1912–1913, architect Paul Mandelstamm). If we turn into Šķūņu Street, we can see a syn-

Corner of Mazā Monētu and Mazā Jaunavu streets

thesis of Art Nouveau and Neo-Classicism in Arenstam's shop building at Šķūņu Street 4 (1911, architect Paul Mandelstamm).

Right next door is the "Flower Building" — a former warehouse at **the corner of Mazā Monētu and Mazā Jaunavu streets**. The facade dates back to the early 20th century, when a drugstore was located in the building. At one time this corner of Old Rīga was

particularly distinguished by the nearby "Jaksch & Co." retail building, which was designed by Karl Johann Felsko in 1900 and had a metal carcass construction and ornate mosaic-type facade decorations designed by architect from Nuremberg T. Eirihs. The building was destroyed during World War II, and today we can look at it only in photographs.

Šķūņu Street 10/12. Detail of the facade

At **Šķūņu Street 10/12** we find the apartment and shop building of Heinrich Dettmann (1903, architects Heinrich Scheel, Friedrich Scheffel) with large display of windows on the bottom floor and a powerful and distinctive bay. There were apartments on the upper floors of the building, while Dettmann's optics shop was located on the ground floor. Dettmann was a successful businessman and one of the owners of the stock company "Union", which worked on behalf of the Berlin company "Siemens" after 1898, and later was turned into the globally known VEF electronics factory. Two of the factory's buildings were put up in 1912 and 1914, designed by the prominent German architect Peter Behrens. Dettmann's shop sold also telephones, which at the time were a true luxury. The facade of the building is decorated with the

Tirgoņu Street 4

Tirgoņu Street 4. Detail of the facade

Tirgoņu Street 4. Detail of the facade

owner's initials and mascarons, but the dominant element comes from nature — chestnut leaves, stalks of grain, daffodils and poppies weave all around the facade. Floral motifs were also used in the interior of the building. Above the bay in the pediment of the building there is the figure of a dog which is "protecting" the building.

Another apartment and shop building of Heinrich Dettmann is located at **Tirgoņu Street 4** (1900, architect Heinrich Scheel, Friedrich Scheffel, W. Hahn). Here we see the powerful impact of Historicism in the decorations of the facade. As journalist Ahrendt Berholz wrote in the early 20th century, the Šķūņu Street building was reminiscent of Belgian Art Nouveau, while the facade of the Tirgoņu Street building was decorated with techniques that were popular in the architecture of Berlin.

Jauniela 25/29

The apartment and shop building of a construction magnate Ludvigs Neiburgs at **Jauniela 25/29** was built after a design by Wilhelm Bockslaff in 1903. Art Nouveau and Historism compete for attention in the facade of the building. The structure seems to be too large in comparison to its surroundings, even though the facade is divided up into several architectonically different segments. The visual impression is created by the monumental mascaron with the image of the sun which adds a heavy but undeniably effective character to the portal of the building.

Evidence of the era of Art Nouveau can also be

Dome Square

Dome Square 8. Detail of the facade

found in buildings that were not put up at the turn of the century. It refers to the Dome Cathedral, for instance, the foyer interior of which acquired some Art Nouveau features after the project of architect Wilhelm Neumann.

In the Dome Square, however, we should focus our attention on two buildings from the early 20th century which help us to understand the way in which Rīga's urban environment was assembled by means of different stylistic techniques. The former building of the Riga Commercial Bank at **Dome Square 8**, which now houses Radio Latvia (1913, architect Paul Man-

Dome Square

Smilšu Steet 1/3. Detail of the facade

delstamm), has sculptures and an allegorical composition in its pediment which were made at the decorative sculpture workshop of August Volz.

The building at **Smilšu Street 1/3** was designed by St.Petersburg architect Nikolay Proskurnin, in 1906, at the request of the insurance company "Rossija". The allegorical figure of Hope at the corner of the building was made at the decorative sculpture workshop of Ferdinand Vlassak where all of the other decorations on the building are likely to have come from —

including the fairly eclectic interior design involving a powerful element of Neo-Classicism.

A small but delicate accent in the story of the synthesis of Art Nouveau and Neo-Classicism in Rigensian buildings is provided by the building at Jēkaba Street 6/8 (1907, architect Hermann Seuberlich). The facade of the former Russian Foreign Trade Bank depicts the aforementioned rod of Hermeus — one of the most successful stylizations of the caduceus motif in the facades of Rīga's buildings.

Smilšu Street 2

If your walk takes place on a weekday, turn into the coffee store at Mazā Pils Street 6, which is owned by the consistory of the Latvian Lutheran Church. Take a cup of coffee in the cozy interior which has been reconstructed several years ago (1996, architect Liesma Markova) and enjoy the presence of authentical Art Nouveau furniture.

Stamm's apartment and shop building at **Smilšu Street 2** (1902, architect Konstantīns Pēkšēns) is the result of the rebuilding of an older structure, but the facade is a testimony to the "Biological Romanticism" of Art Nouveau. The small bay of the building is decorated with a representation of a peacock that was one of the symbols of Art Nouveau — a testament to beauty and pride. The bay is supported on trees with trunks that turn into the figures of an atlas and a caryatid while the roots form a decorative and expressive linear drawing, thus symbolizing the idea of

27

Aldaru Street 2a/Smilšu Street 8

metamorphosis in the composition (something that was typical of Art Nouveau). The reliefs depict various hybrid beings, while the mansard windows are decorated with the symbol of the sun — a sign of restoration and flourishing. A certain reference to Medieval art (Medieval art, as we know, was seen as one of the sources of inspiration for Art Nouveau) is the variation of the subject of a "protector of the building" — in this case these are mascarons with the representation of a dog in the upper part of the bay.

Aldaru Street 2a/Smilšu Street 8. Detail of the entrance hall

Detail of the facade

Ideas and symbols that were typical of Art Nouveau are also seen effectively on Bobrov's residential, shop and office building at **Aldaru Street 2a/ Smilšu Street 8** (1902, architect Heinrich Scheel, Friedrich Scheffel, decorative sculptures by "Otto & Wassil", figures produced by the workshop of August Volz). The building is richly ornated with elements of decorative sculpture — mascarons, hybrid forms, floral motifs and two female nudes above the side bay with a wreath in outstretched hands. Despite the wealth of various decorations, however, the building leaves a harmonic impression.

Both portals are decorated with a typically melancholy female mascaron with closed eyes. The image of the woman was particularly popular in Art Nouveau, usually shown deep in melancholy contemplation or involved in dynamic and accented movements, emphasized through flowing hair and clothing and putting and accent on the aspect of sensitivity, too.

At one time this building was lit up by a statue of a woman up on the roof holding a torch-shaped electric light in an uplifted hand — somewhat reminiscent of the Statue of Liberty in the United States. That figure, like the figures of Atlas in Teātra Street, came from the workshop of August Volz.

Smilšu Street 3

The vestibule of the building is almost a textbook example of Art Nouveau design in Latvia. The scene resembles an arbor, but — as usual in Art Nouveau — not directly. It represents a multi-faceted celebration of the organic world and stylistically melds with the decor on the facade of the building. All of the interiors in the building were once very ornate, although rooms in the various apartments were done up in different styles, as the fashion of the time demanded. Bobrov's building is not only a magnificent example of the architecture and interior design of the turn of the century, it is also one of the buildings in Old Rīga which has successfully

been restored and preserved by its owner, the company "Latio" (renovation in 2000 by AIG and the "Arhiss" architectural firm).

On the opposite side of the street, at **Smilšu Street 3**, there is a building of the former North Bank (1910, architects Arthur Moedlinger and Hermann Seuberlich) which now houses another — the Parex Bank. The portal on the Smilšu Street side is crowned by realistic and plastically expressive figural reliefs that came from the workshop of August Volz and provide a look at the bank as an international institution.

On the corner of Smilšu Street and Basteja Bou-

Photo album. Late 19th–early 20th century. MWTM*

Decorative sculpture. Late 19th–early 20th century. RMHS**

levard (at Vaļņu Street 2), there is a building of the former Agricultural Mutual Aid Society of the Vidzeme Province of the Russian Empire (1911, architect Edgar Friesendorff). The facade of the building includes one of the most artistically expressive late Art Nouveau reliefs in Rīga. The reliefs in the central portal are carved of copper and depict images from antique mythology revealing the basic iconographic idea of the building — the flow of human life, health, the goals which people have and the fruitful work which they do.

In Old Rīga we can obtain our first impression not only of the way in which the old city was built up in the late 19th and early 20th century, but also of the specifics of Art Nouveau architecture in Rīga. Museums that are located in the territory of Old Rīga — the Rīga Museum of History and Shipping, the Museum of Writing, Theater and Music, the Museum of Decorative and Applied Arts, the Latvian Museum of Photography — have collections containing many Art Nouveau objects. You can have a possibility to see several other buildings put up at the turn of the 19th and 20th centuries, as well as to enrich your excursion by visiting the Mentzendorf and Reitern buildings, that will give you a notion about the living space of a rich Rigensian over the course of several centuries and in the turn of the 19th and 20th centuries.

*MWTM — the Museum of Writing, Theater and Music
**RMHS — the Rīga Museum of History and Shipping

Zither. Late 19th–early 20th century. MWTM

Bastejkalns

THE RING OF BOULEVARDS

Aspazijas Boulevard–Bastejkalns–Raiņa Boulevard–
Inženieru Street–Vērmanes Garden–Merķeļa Street–
the building of the Latvian Association–Krišjāņa Barona
Street–Elizabetes Street–the Esplanade–Krišjāņa Valdemāra
Street–Kronvalda Park–Kalpaka Boulevard–Krišjāņa
Valdemāra Street–the State Museum of Art

A specific role in the story of Art Nouveau in Rīga is played by the so-called "ring of boulevards" which encircles Old Rīga, therefore we are starting our second walk at the point where we ended the first one — near Bastejkalns Hill which was one of the most popular places for relaxation in the late 19th and early 20th century's Rīga.

Bastejkalns Hill was made at the location of the former Sand Bastion, and from the top of the hill we can view a scene which perhaps allows us best to understand the enormous importance of the ring of boulevards in the sense of urban construction.

The ring of boulevards was established when the fortifications of Medieval Old Rīga were torn down between 1857 and 1863. The work was supervised by the city's chief architect, Johann Daniel Felsko, and Otto Dietze. The territory which had once been the site of ramparts and other fortifications became a zone for major buildings, boulevards and parks. The main element in the composition is the green area around the city canal which encloses old Rīga in a semi-circle.

The city canal which winds also through Bastejkalns Hill itself was developed on the basis of the old moat of the fortifications. Parks and gardens were installed around it under the supervision of, and the director of Rīga's parks and gardens, Georg Kuphaldt. In 1898, according to his project stone arrangements with small cascades were made on the slope of Bastejkalns Hill, and a stream with small waterfalls was also installed. These elements, albeit in slightly different form, can still be seen today. The footbridge is in the same place where it has been since 1883 — first made of wood, then — of stone (1892, engineer Adolf Agthe). The right bank of the canal provides a romantic view of a Japanese-style summer home for swans. It was designed by Heinrich Scheel and built in 1893 (restored in 2001), and it has been used to house swans that were originally donated by the Rīga Association for Bird Raising. Today we know that the

Latvian National Opera

swan was one of the central elements of Art Nouveau design, and it seems quite apt that the swan found a home in the very center of Rīga on the eve of the Art Nouveau era.

The ring of boulevards was developed in the latter half of the 19th century, and the architectural principles of Historicism are seen there, complete with their "neutral" nature. Architecture in the style of Historicism is cool and nobly impersonal and such are also the buildings in Aspazijas Boulevard and Raiņa Boulevard (the former First City (German) Theater, now the **Latvian National Opera** (1860-1863, architect Ludwig Bohnstedt; reconstruction 1887, architect Reinhold Schmaeling; the fountain in front of the opera was designed by August Volz), in Kalpaka Boulevard and other places. The piety and tolerance toward historical styles characteristic of the school of Historiscim were preserved during the Art Nouveau period to a certain extent, but they did take on a different tone.

In the late 19th century, the interiors of buildings along the ring of boulevards were affected by new fashions, although even around 1900 the people who lived in those buildings viewed Art Nouveau with considerable caution, albeit with some interest. There

Latvian National Opera. Detail of the facade

Sergey Eisenstein in his parents apartment.
1902

Krišjāņa Valdemāra Street 6

were several individual family homes along the ring of boulevards — the former Pfab building at Barona Street 12 (1876, architects Hermann Ende and Wilhelm Boeckmann), for example, and a number of educational institutions — the building which now houses the University of Latvia (1866, architect Gustav F. A. Hilbig), the present Latvian Academy of Music (1873–1875, architect Jānis Frīdrihs Baumanis), etc. Baumanis, incidentally, also designed the Salamonski Circus (1889). Most of the buildings along the ring of boulevards, however, were apartment buildings, and Art Nouveau became really popular in interior design in those buildings in the earliest part of the 20th century.

The building at **Krišjāņa Valdemāra Street 6**, on the corner of Raiņa Boulevard, has a plaque on an exterior wall which bears witness to the fact that the legendary film director Sergey Eisenstein once lived there. His father was the civil engineer Mikhail Eisenstein, whose name is forever written in the history of Art Nouveau architecture in Rīga.

The ring of boulevards also includes **Vērmanes Garden**, which is one of the most popular parks in Rīga and has enjoyed this status since its opening in 1817. The park is named after Anna Gertrud Woehrmann, who donated the land for it, and she is memorialized with a small obelisk. A number of recreational buildings have been put up in the park over the decades, among them a concert stage (1878). Advertising in old newspapers suggests that in the late 19th and

Riga Latvian Association

early 20th century it was often the scene for concerts by military and brass bands. During the winter there was an ice skating rink in front of the stage. A res-taurant was opened in the park in 1872 and remained popular until the early 20th century, when its interior was redesigned in accordance with the modern age. In

Janis Rozentāls. Decorative frieze of the Rīga Latvian Association building. Triptych

the last years of the 19th century the park was also the site of various public events such as hot air balloon demonstrations and jumping out of the balloons with "falling umbrellas".

There were various active public organizations in Rīga in the latter half of the 19th century and the early part of the 20th century and the larger ones put up their own buildings. A key example of early 20th century architecture and of philanthropy at that time is the building of the temperance organization "Ziemeļ-blāzma", which was built in 1910 by the businessman Augusts Dombrovskis in the Mīlgrāvis district of Rīga. Another great structure is **the building of the Rīga Latvian Association**, which was established in 1868. The building was put up in 1909 by the architects Ernests Pole and Eižens Laube, to replace a wooden building which had burned down. The building's style is based on Neo-Classicism, but the powerful influence of Art Nouveau can also be seen. The synthesis

between Neo-Classicism and Art Nouveau which can be seen also in the mosaic-type decorations designed by Janis Rozentāls. The Rīga Latvian Association was established to defend the identity of ethnic Latvians, and so the building's form and Neo-Classical decorations, had to symbolize the link between Latvians as a cultural nation and the classical cultural traditions of Europe.

Many of the interiors have been restored, and the building which during the Soviet occupation was used by Soviet military officers for various cultural activities, now has regained its original glory. Tours of the interior are available with advance notice, and visitors can look at the different interiors that were developed when the building was first put up and then later, when architect Eižens Laube designed a reconstruction in the latter half of the 1930s. It is interesting and instructive to see how within the framework of one — Neo-Classical — theme the interior decorations

Latvian National Library

acquired features characteristic of different eras — refinement of Art Nouveau in the choice of motifs and nuances of colors and tones in the early 20th century, and after a couple of decades — the symbols of Latvian folklore, typical of the last years before Latvia lost independence.

On three sides Vērmanes Garden is enclosed by buildings in the style of Historicism, although individual structures were built in other styles, mostly Neo-Classicism. The new Neo-Classicist buildings that were put up in the early 20th century meld neatly into the elegant and non-passionate ensemble of Historicism.

Another of Pole's Neo-Classicist buildings from the early 20th century is to be seen on the corner of Elizabetes and Krišjāņa Barona streets in front of Vērmanes Garden. On the facades of the former Rīga Craftsmen Loan Cash (Bank) (1910, now — **the Latvian National Library**) a Corinthian Order is used for the capitals of the Classical Order pilasters, while the ornamental friezes make up an accented yet balanced combination of Classicist ornaments, especially modifications of the horn of plenty. This is a design which was often used in the decorations of Rigensian buildings.

The horn of plenty is primarily known as an attribute of Fortuna in ancient mythology, although there

Brivibas Street 38

are versions on the story. The horn of plenty has also been associated with Pluto, who was the god of wealth in Ancient Greece and often appeared as a small boy.

Also on the facade there are allegorical compositions of figures which include Hermeus, but because of distance these are difficult to see. On the fillings of the side doors of the building small dragons, that have rolled themselves up into a circle, are seen "guarding" the wealth of the house.

On the corner of Elizabetes and Brīvības streets (at **Brīvības Street 38**) there is another former bank building designed by Ernests Pole (1911). The site of the building — on a street corner — awards it a certain majesty, while its decorations that include allegoric figures in oval medallions are reminiscent of those which can be seen on the building at Vaļņu Street 2.

Toward the Orthodox cathedral we find another "island" of green — the Esplanade, which was once

The Riga 700th Anniversary Exibition

The Riga 700th Anniversary Exibition

part of the city's fortifications. In the latter half of the 19th century it was a sandy field with a low fence around it and was used for military training. This was stopped only after lengthy debates among official institutions and complaints of local residents about the dust which the soldiers kicked up. The Orthodox cathedral that is on one side of the park was built by architect Robert Pflug in 1876, and for a long time it was the only building in the Esplanade. In the later part of the 19th century military parades, various other events and exhibitions took place there. In 1901 the city of **Rīga** celebrated its **700th anniversary** with an **industrial exhibition** on the Esplanade. Architects Max Scherwinsky and Alfred Aschenkampf built special

Latvian Ethnographic Exibition. 1896

pavilions for the exhibition. One of the pavilions built by master mason H. Kergalw from the exhibition was moved to the former Strēlnieku Garden, now — Kronvalda Park — which contained various entertainments during the 700th anniversary exhibition, that remained in memory of Rigensians for many years. Architects August Reinberg and Wilhelm Neumann worked with the painter Ernst Tode to establish entertainment facilities called "Old Riga" (in Strēlnieku Garden) and "Venice in Rīga" in the so-called Putnu pļava (Bird Meadow). Both of these "cities" were connected by a bridge across the canal. Descriptions tell us that the entertainment was magnificent — gondola rides accompanied by appropriate music, an opportunity to visit special pubs, various children's rides and even a "Negro village of Dahomey" where people could look at real Africans. A great deal of work went into planning the event, and various catalogues, postcards, press publications and other printed works remain behind to help us better to understand Art Nouveau Rīga at the very beginning of the 20th century.

The name of Strēlnieku (or Riflemen's) Garden is related to the Rīga Association of German Riflemen, which was active in improving the area after the city's fortifications were taken down. Strēlnieku Garden was a closed territory which contained a building for the association and a firing range. Opposite Strēlnieku Garden on the other side of the canal was the "Bird Meadow" that was open to everyone. The name probably relates the bow-and-arrow competitions that had been popular in Rīga and elsewhere in Europe since the Middle Ages. Targets for the marksmen were wooden birds that were put up on high poles. The "Bird Meadow" covered the territory between the city canal and Jēkaba Street. Various entertainments and

Latvian National Theater

Latvian National Theater. Detail of the interior

exhibitions were sited there, too. A particularly important event in terms of Latvian culture was an 1896 ethnographic exhibition. It was related to the 10th All-Russian Congress of Archaeologists, and it was of immense importance in Latvia's cultural history. Konstantīns Pēkšēns designed the pavilions for the exhibition, using the motif of the sun, especially on the entrance gate. It was here that the work of young Latvian artists such as Janis Rozentāls, Jānis Valters, Ādams Alksnis, Vilhelms Purvītis and others was displayed together for the first time.

In 1902, on the corner of what are now Kronvalda Boulevard and Valdemāra Street, the building which housed the Second City (Russian) Theater was opened (now — **Latvian National Theater**, 1900–1902, architect August Reinberg). The theater was designed in the style of the 18th century Classicism of Rīga, the so-called burgher Classicism, so as to emphasize its historical nature, but decorations on the facade include a few elements of Art Nouveau. The decorations were produced in the workshop of August Volz, as well as by the "Otto & Wassil" company, which had become popular since the 700th anniversary exhibition.

Latvian Academy of Art

At Valdemāra Street 2a, in the former territory of the fortress, a representable building of the State Bank (now — the Bank of Latvia) was put up from 1902 to 1905 according to the project of August Reinberg in the style of Italian Renaissance architecture. Nothing less grand would have been appropriate, given the proximity of Old Rīga.

In 1902, the city permitted the construction of **the Rīga School of Commerce** at one corner of the Esplanade (1902–1905, architect Wilhelm Bockslaff).

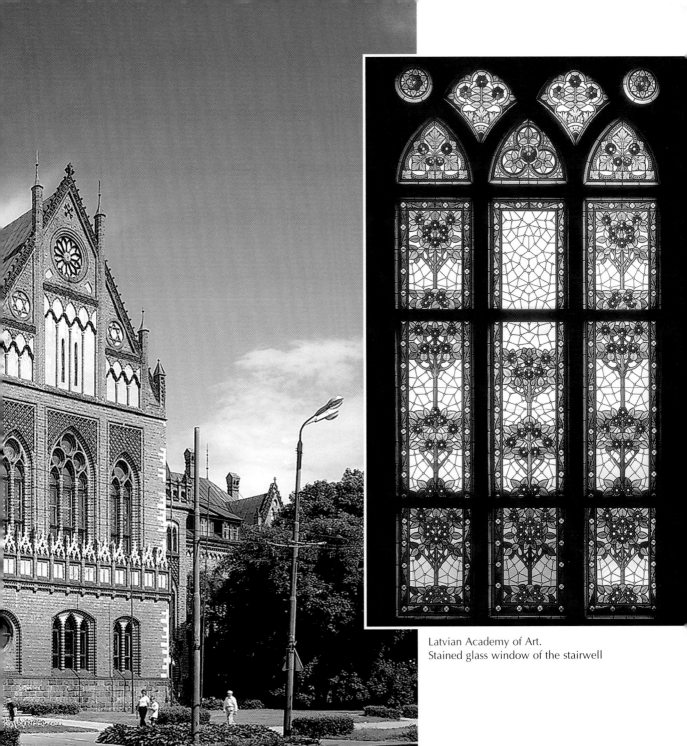

Latvian Academy of Art.
Stained glass window of the stairwell

The building now houses **the Latvian Academy of Art** and was designed in the brick Gothic style so as to emphasize its belonging to Rīga as an ancient Hanseatic city. The interiors, however, show the presence of Art Nouveau — in the rational structure of planning and in several interior decorations, e.g., on the stained glass windows in the stairwell and the meeting hall, at the metal carvings on the banisters, and at the ornate pot-bellied stoves in what were once apartments for the school's teachers.

State Museum of Art

The Rīga City Art Museum (now **the State Museum of Art**) was built by Wilhelm Neumann between 1903 and 1905. It is located alongside the Academy of Art and is Neo-Baroque in form, although decorations include certain elements of Art Nouveau and Neo-Classicism. The decorative sculptures came from the workshop of August Volz.

The figural composition that is on the fronton of the ressault which is broken in Baroque style provides an allegorical representation of various types of art. The rhythm of the composition is subordinated to the curve of the fronton, but the the idea of sculptural sovereignty that is clearly represented in the proportions and the accented plastic volumes testifies to the search of synthesis in the arts that was typical at that period in time. The selection of allegorical representations of the arts points to this, too. At the center of the fronton is Athena — the patron of the arts in antique mythology — with a wreath in her hand, and alongside her we see the Muses of different arts. Perhaps it is precisely because of these sculptures that the subject of artistic allegory became popular in the decoration of other Rīga buildings in the early 20th century.

The entrance to the museum is led by Baroque-like wide stairwell and the heavy doors decorated with metal carvings in Art Nouveau style. The vestibule also contains elements of Art Nouveau in terms of the colors and motifs and in the character of the organization of the space itself. Lunettes on the second floor display landscape motifs that were painted by the Baltic German artist Gerhard von Rosen, as well as the director of the museum, the well-known artist Vilhelms Purvītis; the author of the plastical decorations was August Volz.

The vestibule of the State Museum of Art is where we will complete our second walk through Art Nouveau Rīga. If you wish to obtain a better understanding of the effect of Art Nouveau on the professional arts in Latvia, then buy a ticket at the museum and spend some time with the paintings and sculptures that are displayed therein.

Teodors Zaļkalns. Marble. State Museum of Art

Gustavs Šķilters. Swan's daughter. State Museum of Art

Janis Rozentāls. Spring. State Museum of Art

Andreja Pumpura Street 5

THE CENTRAL DISTRICT I

Andreja Pumpura Street–Jura Alunāna Street–Elizabetes Street–Antonijas Street–Alberta Street–Strēlnieku Street–Elizabetes Street–Rūpniecības Street–Vīlandes Street

The most significant Art Nouveau monuments in Rīga are in the Central District, and this walk is particularly important in learning about the architecture of the period. Buildings here are immensely ornate, in line with the location of the district and the wealth of its residents. On the facades of the structures we see a surprisingly rich palette of artistic and ornamental techniques, with various materials used in the designs.

We begin our walk opposite the Esplanade, entering Pumpura Street from Valdemāra Street. At the first corner, at **Andreja Pumpura Street 5**, we find the monumental Nesterov's apartment building that was built in 1906 and 1907 under the leadership of the

architect Aleksandrs Vanags, although the design was by the Finnish architects Kut Wasastjerna and Gustav Lindberg. The building itself is a testament of sorts to the Finnish art and architecture that were popular in that age, and provided a powerful impulse to the emergence of National Romanticism in Rīga's architecture. We see this in the means of decoration that were used in the building (granite and textured plastering) and in the corner column that was so popular in Nordic architecture. The functional aspects of the building are perfect, but the beautiful, delicate and elegant Art Nouveau interiors were destroyed in nearly all of the building a few years ago.

The proximity of these imposing buildings to the ring of boulevards influenced the architecture of residential buildings in the city's central district. This is seen very clearly in the facades of late Art Nouveau buildings, where designers and architects borrowed liberally from the classical arts. Look at two buildings that are opposite Jura Alunāna Street — **Elizabetes Street 45/47** (1913, architect Artur Moedlinger) and

Elizabetes Street 45/47

Elizabetes Street 41/43 (1913, architect Jānis Alksnis). The elements of style flow together in these buildings, and the classical and Art Nouveau techniques that were used in the facades work together, accenting the contrast between large and small forms, thus reflecting one of the key principles in Art Nouveau compositions.

Along a short stretch of Elizabetes Street, we find three buildings with particularly ornate facades. The oldest is the apartment building of A. Lagzdiņš that was designed in 1901 by the civil engineer Mikhail Eisenstein at **Elizabetes Street 33**. The decor on the facade includes elements of so-called Historic Romanticism, including the so-called principle of *horror vacui* (fear of empty space), as well as certain elements of Art Nouveau. It was in this building that

Elizabetes Street 33

Elizabetes Street 33. Detail of the facade

Eisenstein, while still working on the basis of the principles of Historicism, demonstrated himself to be an architect who could create a unified decorative system not only in the facades of buildings, but also in interiors. He was one of the first architects to reject the idea of having each room in a building done in a different "style". The building is represented in Baranovsky's nine-volume encyclopedia of architecture

Elizabetes Street 10b

Elizabetes Street 10b. Detail of the facade

which was issued in the early 20th century in St. Petersburg.

Two years later, in 1903, Eisenstein designed Lyebedinsky's apartment building at **Elizabetes Street 10b**. It is particularly interesting to us because it represents a unique version of international Art Nouveau. The decor on the facade testifies to a powerful interest in Symbolism. It is a story without beginning and end — the important thing here is a suggestion of hidden content. The appearance of the building has changed over the decades. We see this in a postcard from the early 20th century — the places where the motif of flames appears today used to hold figures of young women with rings in their hands. Eisenstein often used the female figure in a symbolic way, accenting the secretive nature of a woman and often representing her in the context of fantastic images. This particular feature was often seen in the design of mascarons. There, we see unbelievably beautiful women, as well as strange creatures of an indeterminate gender.

Eisenstein's facades contain anthropomorphic, zoomorphic and hybrid beings, as well as abstract and floral motifs. The nature of these compositions — the choice of elements and the overall emotional tone — acquires similarity with the grotesque of Mannerism. The principle of contrast is reflected in the childishly naive little sun under the balcony, contrary to the dramatically significant mood of the whole decor on the facade of the apartment and shop building at **Elizabetes Street 10a** (1903, civil engineer Mikhail Eisenstein).

The apartment and commercial building at **Antonijas Street 8** was designed by the

Elizabetes Street 10a. Detail of the facade

Elizabetes Street 10a. Detail of the facade

Antonijas Street 8. Detail of the facade

architect Konstantīns Pēkšēns in 1903. The portal is decorated by plastically expressive dragons, while the supple appearance of the decorations continues in the ornamental frieze between the first and the second floor. Various interpretations of the dragon theme can also be seen in the upper part of the facade — Pēkšēns often turned to the dragon for inspiration.

Alberta Street 2a

In opposite to the building is a café *Lidojošā varde* (The Flying Frog) — a name that is reminiscent of the "Biological Romanticism" that was part of the style of Art Nouveau. If you would like to visit the café, you can try to determine which of the stained glass windows in the interior are authentic and which ones were created later. Art Nouveau stained glass windows are a rarity in the windows of Rigensian buildings these days. Time has not been kind to many of the build-

ings on the street, including Boguslavsky's apartment building at **Alberta Street 2a** (1906, architect Mikhail Eisenstein). A memorial plaque on the building tells us that the prominent British philosopher Isaiah Berlin lived there from 1909 until 1915.

Alberta Street is unique for its early 20th century Art Nouveau architecture. On the left side of the street there are apartment buildings which were designed by various architects between 1900 and 1908. Design of

Alberta Street 2a. Detail of the facade.

the apartment building at Alberta Street 1 supposedly is created around 1901 by the architects bureau of Heinrich Scheel and Friedrich Scheffel. This one as well as the building at Alberta Street 5 (1900, architect Friedrich Scheffel), followed by the one at Alberta Street 9 (1901, architect Konstantīns Pēkšēns) have facade decors that testify to strong links with Historicism. Niedra's apartment building at **Alberta Street 11**, which was designed by Eižens Laube in 1908, is a vivid example of National Romanticism in Rigensian architecture. The decorative effect was achieved with the delicate use of materials and textures on the facade. Essential is the contrast to the other buildings on the street and their rid plastical decoration, revealing the fact that decorative effect could be achieved with very laconic resources, thus emphasizing the search for "truth" that was typical in the practice and theory of architecture at that time.

The majority of buildings on the right side of the street were apartment houses designed by Mikhail Eisenstein between 1904 and 1906, and belonging to different owners. The saturated decor on the buildings creates the impression of an ensemble, although the buildings are different from those on the ring of boulevards. Each building was designed so as to look

Alberta Street 11

53

Strēlnieku Street 4a

different from the others, and the impression of uniformity in this case is a phenomenon of Art Nouveau.

Glazed brick has been used along with paint on the facades of the buildings. Accent has been laid on contrast of the size of plastical elements, oppositions between voluminous and flat, naturalistically expressed or powerfully stylized. According to the principles of Art Nouveau each element possesses a certain sym-bolic meaning. Of importance are the numerical relationships among the various motifs that were used, as are the forms that were chosen.

Two other Eisenstein buildings can be seen on the opposite side of Alberta Street — Lyebedinsky's apartment building at Alberta Street 13 and Mitu-sov's private school at **Strēlnieku Street 4a** (the corner of Alberta and Strēlnieku streets). Decorations

Alberta Street 13. Detail of the facade

on Eisenstein's buildings tended to be dramatically expressive, and the culmination of this can be seen at **Alberta Street 13**, where the images of the plastical decoration are bestowed an extremely subjective character. Perhaps this was nothing accidental nor the whim of the client especially if we take into account Eisenstein's understanding of conjuncture and his intellectualism as well as the fact that building deco-

rations were developed between 1905 and the beginning of World War I. It is interesting to note that during the Soviet occupation, the building served as the headquarters for a secret military institution — some images of the plastical decoration make one smile at the fact.

The two buildings have undergone significant restoration and reconstruction in the last several years,

Alberta Street 13. Detail of the facade

and both now house educational institutions. By calling ahead one can have an opportunity to look at the interiors of what is now the Rīga School of Law (Alberta Street 13, restoration done by the "Velve" company in 2000 and 2001). The interiors of Eisenstein buildings were based exclusively on Art Nouveau's ornamental forms and stylistically unified ensemble of rooms.

The ensemble along the street is completed by an

Alberta Street 12

apartment building which Konstantīns Pēkšēns and Eižens Laube designed at **Alberta Street 12** in 1903 (Pēkšēns actually owned the building). The appearance of the building, especially its picturesque roof, pro-

vides a nice accent to the Art Nouveau ensemble of Alberta Street. The choice of decorative plastic elements is dominated by motifs of local flora and fauna — pine cones, squirrels, etc, but entering the

The exibit of Janis Rozentāls memorial museum

Janis Rozentāls. Portrait of Elli Rozentāle

stairwell in order to see the ornamentally impressive deco-rations, one has to turn attention to realistical landscape paintings enclosed in lunettes. This was a popular type of decorations in the early years of the 20th century. The finest rooms of the apartments had stained glass windows and delicate plastical decorations, including Apartment 1 on the first floor, where Pēkšēns had his design bureau. The office was typical of the early 20th century, with a fireplace, oak paneling on the walls, and an ornately decorated plafond with the motif of chestnut leaves which surround tense yet, at the same time, relaxed lines of "whip strokes". Many members of the Latvian intelligentsia lived in the building, including the architects Eižens Laube and Aleksandrs Vanags, as well as the writer Rūdolfs Blaumanis. The top floor has been turned into a **memorial museum for the painter Janis Rozentāls**, and a visit to the museum will allow you to learn not only about the artist's work, but also about the specifics of interior design in the early 20th century. The artist himself designed much of the furniture and possibly also the interior for the entire apartment.

Besides the buildings of Alberta Street, there is a number of other buildings in this part of the city, worth of attention, which demonstrate as vast range of expressive techniques. Fischer's apartment building at Strēlnieku Street 6 (1902, architects Konstantīns Pēkšēns and Aleksandrs Vanags), for

Strēlnieku Street 2. Detail of the facade

example, has decorative techniques and motifs which suggest that the work was done by the decorative sculpture firm "Lotze & Stoll".

The apartment and shop building of Miķelis Bruže at **Strēlnieku Street 2** (1911, architect Mārtiņš Nukša), represents the so-called Perpendicular Art Nouveau where the decorative effect is achieved by the accenting of vertical elements throughout the facade. The humbly treated plastical decorations on the upper part of the facade show a stylized representation of a stalk of grain.

Two 1910 buildings on the corner of Strēlnieku and Elizabetes streets are clearly based on the principles of Neo-Classicism (Elizabetes Street 21a, architect Mārtiņš Nukša, and Strēlnieku Street 13, architect Eižens Pole).

Savickis' apartment building at **Elizabetes Street 23** (1903, architect Hermann Otto Hilbig; now houses the Aizkraukles Bank) is an example of early Art Nouveau, with expressive but comparatively reticent decorations which are based on abstract, floral and anthropomorphic designs and an accentuated portal. The ornamental frame in the pediment contains the Latin phrase *Labor omnia vincit* (Work conquers all). This is an example of the aforementioned tendency in the early 20th century when decorations of the building were bestowed a personal

Elizabetes Street 23. Detail of the facade

Elizabetes Street 23

character, pointing to the owner's ethical principles.

At the corner of Elizabetes and Vīlandes Streets — **Vīlandes Street 1** — we see an apartment building which was designed (in 1898) and owned by the architect Rudolf Zirkwitz. The building is one of the most beautiful examples of architecture from the period of late Historicism in Rīga where we see elements of historical styles in conjunction with particular motifs of Art Nouveau. The positive assessment of the building among specialists of the early 20th century is proved by the fact, that its image was published in several specialized publications. The Vīlandes Street facade shows us a variation on decorative sculpture that was popular in Historicism — a beaming mascaron which is placed in a dynamic angle against Vīlandes Street. Above it is a figure which was intended to be an allegorical representation of architecture, thus emphasizing the profession of the owner. The interior design of the building corresponds to the principles of Historicism, however, the Zirkwitz building is important in that we find one of the earliest Art Nouveau interiors in Rīga in it. The vestibule is decorated to remind

Vilandes Street 1

Elizabetes Street 13

us of the 24-hour cycle of the day and night. Art Nouveau influences are particularly clear if we look at the original design (an allegory of the second half of the 19th century) and then compare it to the finished product. Praise for organic life, characteristic of Art Nouveau, is treated with naive directness and sentimentally romantic joyfulness. Today the building is owned by an insurance company "Fēnikss", and interiors have been restored by the company's initiative.

Lazdiņš' apartment building at the corner of Rūpniecības and Elizabetes streets — at **Elizabetes Street 13** — was designed, in 1904, by Konstantīns Pēkšēns. The decorations of the building make clear the functional nucleus of the building. The decor, in line with the principles of Art Nouveau, contrasts decorated areas with plain ones (the so-called *amor vacui* principle), and the elements reflect a variation on the subject of German Renaissance.

Vilandes Street 11. Detail of the facade

Rūpniecības Street provides us with a wealth of Art Nouveau buildings, as does Vīlandes Street, which runs parallel to it. The specifics of buildings and the size of plots of land along the two streets promote the idea of a unified ensemble.

There are several other buildings along Vīlandes Street that were designed by Zirkwitz, and the decoration motifs changed along with the circle of Art Nouveau themes. Bikars' apartment building at **Vīlandes Street 11**, which was designed in 1899 and 1900, was one of the first buildings in Rīga which has a structure and facade decorations that amongst the Neo-Baroque elements of decoration include also Art Nouveau motifs (windows shaped like keyholes, for example), however, maintaining close links to Historicism. In spite of the aspirations to bestow dynamic expression to both shy maidens on the portal decorations, they still remind of those delicately and academically inter-

Vīlandes Street 10

preted figures which are typical of building decorations in Historicism. However the movement of the hands of the two women depicts one of the most popular ways in which beautiful goddesses were shown in antiquity (the so-called *Venus Pudica* appearance).

Several buildings on Vīlandes Street were designed by Konstantīns Pēkšēns, and each is different in terms of its decorations. This is particularly true about those buildings which are from the late Art Nouveau period — buildings which include the accented and rhythmic vertical decorations. The building facade at Vīlandes Street 14 (1909) is based on Perpendicular Art Nouveau but also includes reminiscences of the classical arts, making a free variation on the theme of the Classical Order. Pārups' apartment building at **Vīlandes Street 10** (1908) is surprising in terms of the imagination that was used in its design — the arrangement of its various elements and the decorations, including the use of a half timbering. The relief on the facade shows a depiction of classical art, which indicates that theme-based reliefs were popular in late Art Nouveau buildings.

Vilandes Street 10. Detail of the facade

Vilandes Street 4. Detail of the facade

Bērziņš' apartment building at **Vīlandes Street 4** (1908) includes engraved ornamentation on the facade. At the center of the building there is a stylized female mask, where the ornament is merged with a lightly plastic modelling which links the design to the image that was very popular at the turn of the century — a woman with her eyes closed — thus depicting the theme of secrecy. The popular Latvian sculptor Teodors Zaļkalns were among those artists who resorted to this image in several of his own works.

Kronvalda Boulevard 10

Konstantīns Pēkšēns is seen, with good reason, as one of the most important and imaginative architects in Rīga in the late 19th and early 20th centuries. His work was closely linked to the development of National Romanticism. Pēkšēns worked with the young architects Eižens Laube and Aleksandrs Vanags to put up the first major buildings in the style of National Romanticism in Rīga. At the place where Elizabetes Street crosses Kronvalda Park, at **Kronvalda Boulevard 10**, we find a Pēkšēns and Laube apartment and shop building from 1907 which is a typical example of architecture in the style of National Romanticism. It has an expressive silhouette, an accent on the natural stone structure, and laconic decorations.

This building concludes the third walk during which we had a possibility to clear up architectural features essential of Art Nouveau era in Rīga. The general impression makes a sufficiently strong basis to allow oneself to turn to the numerous and fascinating nuances.

Brivibas Street 55

THE CENTRAL DISTRICT AND NEIGHBOURING SUBURBS

There are far too many architectural monuments from the period of Art Nouveau in the Central District and neighbouring suburbs of Rīga to include them in a single walk. Go in any direction, and you will find buildings of high artistic quality. This is one of the reasons why the historical center of Rīga is on the global heritage list of UNESCO. Let us look at a few specific buildings which are located in various parts of Rīga, and this may be the stimulus to look for the surrounding buildings as well.

If we are to understand the use of early Art Nouveau principles in Rigensian architecture, we must look at the apartment building which was put up in

Krišjāņa Valdemāra Street 23

1900 at **Brīvības Street 55**, designed by the Berlin architect Albert Giesecke and built under the supervision of Wilhelm Neumann. The building is known as the *Büngnerhof*, and its architectonic composition was adapted for many other buildings in Rīga in subsequent years. The choice of the plastic elements of the facade demonstrate retrospectiveness, and interaction of Historicism and Art Nouveau has determined also the building's interior design.

Fantastic images and themes in the context of the "Biological Romanticism" can be seen in Savickis'

apartment building at **Krišjāņa Valdemāra Street 23** (1901, architects Heinrich Scheel and Friedrich Scheffel, with facade sketches by Albert Giesecke), as well as in Tupikov's apartment building at Ģertrūdes Street 10/12 (1902, architects Heinrich Schell and Friedrich Scheffel, with decorative sculptures by "Otto & Wassil"). The construction forms in the facade decor are dynamically balanced so as to emphasize change and the ability of "transformation". The building at Ģertrūdes Street 10/12, for example, has an "expressive" mascaron with a beard that turns into march

Brivibas Street 68. Detail of the facade

marigold blossoms, while another mascaron has a beast on either side, along with the trident that was a main prop for the mythical figure of Poseidon. Photographs of the building from the early 20th century show a group of sculptures at the top of the structure which have not survived.

The use of fantastic images involved a unique solution at another decoratively impressive apartment buildings from this period at **Tallinas Street 23** (1901, architects Konstantīns Pēkšēns and Eižens Laube, decorative sculptures by "Lotze & Stoll"). The ending of the bay together with the entrance portal resemble the open jaws of a dragon. Various images of dra-gons were also used in other buildings — the apartment and shop building at **Blaumaņa Street 28** (1903, architect Karl Johann Felsko), for example. One of the most "photogenic" dragons can be found on the facade of the apartment building at Lāčplēša Street 24. The facade of the apartment building at Lāčplēša Street 100 provides another aspect of the world of fantastic images — witches, in this case.

Tallinas Street 23

Blaumaņa Street 28. Detail of the facade

Aleksandra Čaka Street 26. Detail of the facade

Tērbatas Street 15/17. Detail of the facade

Tērbatas Street 15/17

One of the most distinguished pages in early 20th century architecture in Rīga is connected with National Romanticism. Kļaviņa's apartment building at **Aleksandra Čaka Street 26** (1905, architects Konstantīns Pēkšēns and Eižens Laube) is one of the oldest examples of National Romanticism in Rīga. The stylized ornaments in the facade of the building are enhanced by the expressive phrase in Latvian *Mans nams — mana pils* ("My home is my castle").

Atis Ķeniņš' school building at **Tērbatas Street 15/17** (1905, architects Konstantīns Pēkšēns and Eižens Laube) has various contrasting textures on

Krišjāņa Valdemāra Street 67

the facades, as well as typical sloped window forms which are early examples of National Romanticism in Rīga. This involved an effort to reject the international elements of Art Nouveau. The choice of the materials which were used on the facade is also symbolic —

according to architecture historian Jānis Krastiņš, the travertine came from the fabled Staburags cliff, which was submerged under the waters of the Daugava River when a hydroelectric dam was built nearby.

An ensemble of buildings which will help us bet-

Brivibas Street 58

ter to understand National Romanticism is the impressive set of structures in Krišjāņa Valdemāra Street designed by Eižens Laube (the apartment and shop building at **Krišjāņa Valdemāra Street 67**, 1909) and Aleksandrs Vanags (the apartment buildings at Krišjāņa Valdemāra Street 69 (1909) and at Krišjāņa Valdemāra Street 71 and 73 (1910)). Several buildings can be seen in Brīvības Street — Brigaders' apartment

Brivibas Street 47

and shop building at **Brīvības Street 58** (1906, architect Aleksandrs Vanags), Krastkalns' apartment and shop building at **Brīvības Street 47** (1908, architect Eižens Laube), Freijs' apartment and shop building at Brīvības Street 37 (1909, architect Eižens Laube), and others.

Many artistically expressive buildings are related to the later period of Art Nouveau — Savickis' apartment building at Baznīcas Street 5 (1907, architect Friedrich Scheffel), for example, is notable for its elaborate plastical appearance. The vertical aspects of the facade are balanced out by more gentle forms and by the modest decor. Scheffel also designed the Red Cross hospital at Asara Street 3 (1910).

Tērbatas Street 14

The building of the Rīga Traders Mutual Credit Society Bank, shops and apartments at **Tērbatas Street 14** (1909, architects Konstantīns Pēkšēns and Arthur Moedlinger) has an expressive silhouette — the use of high-quality stone decoration materials has determined the building's modest yet noble appearance.

Ornamental and gilded reliefs at the corner of the building depict variations on the theme of the caduceus, appropriately for the functions of the structure. Stained glass windows by Kārlis Brencēns can still be seen in the interior of the building. The subjects which Brencēns treated in his windows helped Latvians to

Brivības Street 33

develop their national self-esteem, just like the mosaic which Janis Rozentāls produced for the facade of the Latvian Association building.

The Rīga Traders and Manufacturers Mutual Credit Society Bank at **Brīvības Street 33** (1912, architect Eižens Laube) is a successful example of Perpendicular Art Nouveau with distinctly vertical composition, that has dictated the basic approach to the decorations on the building. The laconic plastic decorations on the pediment involve a stylized representation of stalks of grain thus replacing the traditional symbols that were used to decorate buildings of a similar kind.

The language of symbols characteristic of Art Nouveau could at times reflect the ethical principles of the owners of the buildings. Forms, however, could be very varied — depending on the taste of those who commissioned the projects.

The example to the above mentioned is the apartment building of architect Augusts Reinbergs at **Skolas Street 3** (1905, architect Augusts Reinbergs). The facade has accented textural contrasts and a romantic balcony above which there is a stylized depiction of rose blossoms. Under the balcony there is a figural relief which tells a story that relates to the profession of the building's owner. The text speaks to the same idea, and the side facade has a decorative motif with a graphic depiction of musical notes. In this case the meaning can be explained in two ways — it may be the music was seen as a key priority in the arts of the day, or it may depict the favorite leisure activities of the building owner.

Skolas Street 12a. Detail of the facade

Skolas Street 3

The building at **Skolas Street 12a** (1908, architect E. Buśs) shows one of the most unusual portal decorations in Rīga. On one side of the gate there is the figure of a sitting human being, while on the opposite side there is an ape-like figure. We can only guess whether this speaks to the role of work in human evolution or whether some other subjective consideration came into play.

Matisa Street 40/42

Decor on the facades of buildings in the later period of Art Nouveau often included various aspects of antique arts. This was often true with respect to buildings which were designed by the architect Jānis Alksnis. The apartment building at **Matīsa Street 40/42** (1908), for example, shows Heracles in battle with the lion of Nemea. At Marijas Street 18 (1908), we find three reliefs at the center of the facade with various antique heroes — Atlas, Heracles and Prometheus.

The realistic depiction of these mythical figures illustrates the tensely emotional nature of the decorative arts at the turn of the 19th and 20th centuries. In this case, the figures may also reflect certain social ideals.

Clear "quotes" from the classical arts are also found on the facade of the building at Ģertrūdes Street 60 (1908, architect Rudolf Dohnberg). The relief at the center of the facade is based on a painting by the 17th century Italian artist Guido Reni (1575–1642), "Aurora

Lāčplēša Street 61

Scattering Blossoms". On the facade of the building at **Lāčplēša Street 61** (1909, architect Rudolf Dohnberg), there is a relief which shows the gods of Mount Olympus, alongside various allegorical depictions of the arts. Allegories became popular in the late period of Art Nouveau, when the influence of Neo-Classicism became stronger. The arts were often the subject of these allegories. We see this in the sandstone brick reliefs that are on the facade of Virsis' apartment building at Brīvības Street 62 (1908, architect Eižens Laube). The allegories supplement the abstract ethnographic motifs that were used in the ornamental decor of the building. One of the figures symbolizes architecture, while the other depicts sculpture.

The aforementioned buildings are only a small part of the whole architectural heritage the notion of which can be widened by more extensive excursions into the former suburbs.

Pārdaugava. Early 20th century postcard

PĀRDAUGAVA

Slokas Street–the Theater Museum–Eduarda Smiļģa Street–Daugavgrīvas Street–Buļļu Street–Dzegužu Street–Dzegužkalns Hill–Buļļu Street–Daugavgrīvas Street–the Gustavs Šķilters Museum–Meža Street–Nometņu Street–Slokas Street–Mārtiņa Street–Alises Street–Kristapa Street–Kalnciema Street–Nometņu Street–the Āgenskalns Market–Mārupes Street–the Stradiņš Clinical University Hospital–the Māras Pond–Ojāra Vācieša Street–Arkādijas Park–Torņakalna Street–the Torņakalns viaduct–the Torņakalns Church–Vienības Alley–the Georg Armitsted Children's Clinical University Hospital–Jelgavas Street–Kuģu Street

The Pārdaugava region is situated on the left bank of the Daugava River, and until the beginning of the 20th century it was known as the Jelgava Suburb of the city. It was the last of the city's districts to be built up, and it was attached to the city of Rīga only in the late 18th century. The first settlements sprang up around river crossing facilities where roads from Zemgale, Kurzeme and Daugavgrīva approached the river. Because of the frequent floods in the Daugava the area until the early 17th century was poorly populated. Three villages emerged — the precursors to what are now the Torņakalns, Āgenskalns and Iļģuciems neighborhoods of Rīga. Most of the residents came from the rural environment, and they worked as anchor men, sorters of trees for masts, fishermen, cart drivers and the owners of boats which carried people across the river.

Much of the land around Rīga belonged to so-called "mini-estates", where the city's rich (mostly Ger-

mans) spent their summers. There were some 60 mini-estates in Pārdaugava, and the system flourished in the 18th and early 19th century. As population numbers in the city's suburbs increased and the nearby Jūrmala seashore became more popular, the mini-estates lost their importance. Pārdaugava began to grow most rapidly in the latter half of the 19th century. Several factories were sited there, and three rail lines crossed the territory. Separate areas of old construction and the picturesque vicinity, however, remained untouched, and Pārdaugava maintained its importance as a leisure area even in the late 19th and early 20th century. This was particularly true of the Āgenskalns neighborhood, where many people had had summer homes since the mid-19th century. There was a pier at Āgenskalns, and boat and ship traffic along the Daugava was intensive until the early 20th century, with several shipping lines competing for business.

Traffic between the two banks of the Daugava River had always been a problem. A bridge for pedestrians and horse-drawn carriages was put up in 1873, and it continued to be used for foot traffic until a railroad line was put across the bridge. A pontoon bridge designed by Adolf Agthe was installed in 1896 to replace an old and very unsafe raft bridge. Until the early 20th century one could ride a sleigh across the frozen water of the river during the wintertime. After 1908, some private businesses began to offer automobile transportation across the ice.

As Pārdaugava became more industrialized in the latter half of the 19th century, population numbers increased. Multi-story stone apartment buildings appeared in Pārdaugava, just like in other parts of Rīga, and Art Nouveau became a part of its architecture in the early 20th century. Designs for these buildings were produced by the city's well-known architectural firms. Art Nouveau buildings in Pārdaugava have to be surveyed in order to understand one of the most important aspects of Rigensian architecture — the precise comprehension of the environment. As was the case in other former suburbs, buildings in Pārdaugava had certain specifics of decoration, where traditions of craftsmanship often dominated over the sculptural professionalism. This last fact makes the buildings in Pārdaugava particularly attractive. There are also, however, several buildings which evidence a very delicate approach to style. The size of apartment buildings in Pārdaugava also makes the area different from the city center — they are smaller and more "intimate".

One of such apartment buildings is located at **Eduarda Smiļģa Street 10** (1904, architect Jānis Alksnis). The building is not particularly fancy, but the facade is one of the most interesting examples of

Eduarda Smilga Street 10. Detail of the facade

Meža Street 4a. Detail of the facade

decorations which Alksnis produced in the early period of Art Nouveau. Several of the buildings in Eduarda Smilǵa Street were put up in the late 19th and early 20th century.

Around the Orthodox Church of the Holy Trinity (1891–1895, architect Vladimirs Lunskis) at Meža Street 2, we find several apartment buildings from the early 20th century which have an appearance that speaks to the style of Historism but also includes certain elements of Art Nouveau.

Pečaks' apartment and shop building at **Meža Street 4a**, which was built between 1900 and 1903 after a design by Konstantīns Pēkšēns, is one of the most unique Neo-Gothic buildings in Rīga. The portal which faces the church is worth a look. The two mascarons are variations on the subject of the dragon —

Meža Street 4

a protector of buildings and a subject which Pēkšēns used very often. The idea of "Biological Romanticism" is represented by the peculiar crab-like creatures, while the decor is made all the more amusing by the fact that it was produced by craftsmen, not sculptors.

The building at **Meža Street 4**, which was de-signed by the architect Mārtiņš Nukša in 1912, along-side the elements of Neo-Classicism and use of the order theme in reliefs, contains motifs that are typical of Art Nouveau — local flora, peacocks, an owl, the interpretation of which includes also rusticalized elements.

Daugavgrivas Street 74/76

The apartment and shop building at **Daugavgrī-vas Street 74/76** (1907, architect Jānis Alksnis) is one of the most impressive buildings in the neighborhood. To compensate the dimensions of the long and relatively low facade, the weighty building is divided into several blocs. The decor involves reliefs with images from antique mythology (analogous images can be seen in an Alksnis-designed building at Matīsa Street 40/42) and other stylistic motifs. The pediments are topped by figures of bears, and there are also certain heraldic motifs with the aim to create an impression of ceremony. The compositions of the

Dzegužkalns on an early 20th century postcard and today

pediments were probably arranged on the basis of a lower perspective, because the effect seems a bit exaggerated when we look at it today.

Several parks were installed in Pārdaugava in the late 19th and early 20th century. Among them **Dzeguž-kalns** which is one of the most beautiful parks in Rīga, famed for its beautiful landscaping and the highest hill in Rīga (28 meters above sea level). The park was designed by landscape designer Georg Kuphaldt in 1900, and enormous work was involved. Earth was brought in by horse-drawn cart from the distant meadows at Spilve. The park was completed in 1911, and a small coffee pavilion was installed at the top of the hill.

Pārdaugava is the place in Rīga where one can still enjoy the quiet atmosphere of a suburb, complete with trees and lilac bushes. Old and twisting streets that have survived till nowadays are named after various aspects of nature — bees (Bišu Street), honey (Medus), the forest (Meža), the finch (Žubīšu).

Evidence of the old summer homes can still be seen quite clearly in Daugavgrīvas Street, as can one of the oldest churches in Pārdaugava — the St. Martin's Church, which was built in 1851 and 1852 after a design by Johann Daniel Felsko and then rebuilt in 1887 after a design by Heinrich Scheel. The building was supposedly financed through donations that were collected after a tragedy in the spring of 1850, when several dozen people who were heading for worship services in Inner Rīga drowned when the ice of the Daugava River broke in below them.

A building that belonged to the architect Alfred Aschenkampf (1903) is at **Daugavgrīvas Street 32/34**, and alongside it, at Daugavgrīvas Street 36 (1912, architect E. Laube), is a building with one of the most unusual tile panels in the vestibule from early 20th century Rīga, with landscape illustrations at the center.

The residential building at **Nometņu Street 5** (1911, architect Jānis Alksnis) is distinguished by its

Nometņu Street 5

expressive appearance. The ornate decor on the building is a testament to the fact that architects who worked in the period of late Art Nouveau sought out inspiration in historical styles, and that the role of the language of symbols was gradually loosing its significance.

The building at Slokas Street 16 (1908, architect Wilhelm Roessler), which used to house the city's pawn shop, now is home to the State Historical Archive. It has a distinct silhouette and geometric decorations on the pediment which are typical of late Art Nouveau.

Slokas Street 31

The official nature of the building led the designers to include elements of Russia's imperial eagle and the official seal of the city of Rīga in the design. This gives the building a serious, even slightly threatening appearance.

The residential building at Slokas Street 29/1 was designed by the architect Aleksandrs Vanags in 1911, and the architectonic solution and facade decor that were used are another indication of the search for historical inspiration in the late period of Art Nouveau. Blaus' apartment building at Slokas Street 31 (1908, architect Konstantīns Pēkšēns) displays certain ele-

ments of National Romanticism, as well as stylized and decorative Order motifs. The facade on the side of Mārtiņa Street is decorated with small dragons done in metal.

Several Art Nouveau-inspired residential buildings can be found in Mārtiņa and Alises streets. Looking at these buildings one can see how specific interpretation of stylistic issues is localized in a particular area, and how techniques and decorative motifs "migrated" from one area to another. The same is true in the area of Kapseļu Street and elsewhere.

Alises Street 5. Detail of the facade

The residential building at **Alises Street 5** (1913, architect Edgar Friesendorff) is a typical building from the late period of Art Nouveau. Construction principles of this apartment building are close to those of single family homes. The reliefs on the facade show patriarchal and idyllic images which focus on the process of labor and two birds who are "carefully tending" to their nest.

As the population of Rīga increased, there ap-peared new demands for reformation of water supply and sewage systems. The city began to install a new water pipeline in the early 20th century, and it went on line in 1904. **The water tower at Āgenskalns**, which was built in 1910 after a design by Wilhelm Bockslaff, is a brilliant example of the synthesis of international Art Nouveau and local forms. The entrance above the portal is topped by a geometric ornament, enclosed in a triangular tympanum. As in the pawn shop building

Water tower at Āgenskalns. Detail of the facade

that was discussed above, the ornament stylizes imperial eagles and the city seal. The emotional effect here, however, is different.

Nearby, at Margrietas Street 16, is one of the earliest buildings of Mikhail Eisenstein where powerful influence of Historicism can still be observed. In this area of Āgenskalns there are several apartment and shop buildings that were put up at the end of the 19th and at the beginning of the 20th century which testify to the influence of Art Nouveau in their construction forms as well as facade decorations.

Nometņu Street 47

On the corner of Lapu and Nometņu streets, at **Nometņu Street 47**, is a building of contractor J.Feld-manis (1909, architect Wilhelm Bockslaff) which is one of the most vivid examples of National Romanticism in Pārdaugava. The half-timbering on the upper floor of the building is both of practical and decorative im-portance. Along with the carefully considered colors of the building, it serves to make the structure appear smaller and more appropriate for its surroundings.

One of the most beautiful early Art Nouveau buildings in Rīga can be found at **Nometņu Street 45**. We don't know who designed it or when it was com-pleted, but it is undoubtedly a contemporary of the buildings which Heinrich Scheel and Friedrich Scheffel designed at Smilšu Street 8 and Ģertrūdes Street 10/12. It is likely that the delicate and beautiful decorations on the building, with lily blossoms and mascarons, came from the "Otto & Wassil" company. The unusual roof of the building calls to mind the early Renais-sance castles of France. The decor surely does not sym-bolize the fate of the building — the Pre-Raphaelitic-ally beautiful mascaron is surrounded by snakes, making it similar to the mythological monster Medusa Gorgona, who made anyone who looked at her turn into stone.

Nometņu Street 45. Detail of the facade

The Āgenskalns Market at Nometņu Street 65 was built, beginning
in 1911, after a design by the architect
Reinhold Schmaeling. The building was
completed only after World War I.
Schmaeling, who was the chief architect of Rīga from 1879 until 1917, was
an outstanding master of the brick
style whose buildings have certain
elements of Art Nouveau in their design. When Rīga Mayor George Armitsted launched an extensive program of
school building, Schmaeling designed
several sample schools. Each of the 15
buildings that were put up was based
on one of the designs, but with variations within the theme. One such building is found at Zeļļu Street 4 (1910).

Arkādijas Park, which was known
as Torņakalna Park until 1910, was
taken over by the city in 1896. The
park was opened to the public in
1898, and it soon became popular.
Georg Kuphaldt worked out a design
which involved a change in the direction of the Mārupīte River so that it
would become a part of the park's
structure. The stream was diverted into
the central part of the park, and several small cascades and a miniature
waterfall was arranged on it.

A new restaurant was built near
the park in 1910, called "Arkādija", or
Arcadia. The name of the fabled region
of Ancient Greece was soon given also
to the park. The park was a very popular leisure site, and fire fighters, choirs,

Arkādijas Park

musical organizations and other groups of people loved
to stage celebrations there. Open-air performances,
concerts and competitions took place there as well.
The picturesque vicinity around the Māras Pond helped
to make the park popular. The pond had borrowed its
name from Māras or Svētās Māras (St. Mary's) Mill, that
was located on the site from the 13th century.

Zeļļu Street 4

Torņakalna viaduct

Vienības Gatve, which used to be known as the Jelgava highway, was partly built up at the turn of the 19th and 20th century, yet at Vienības Gatve 29 and 31 we find buildings which Eižens Laube designed in 1912. The apartment and shop buildings contain certain elements of Art Nouveau, but without a distinctly individual solution in either case. These are typical suburban buildings — stolid and at the edge of districts where working class people lived. The structures are not unnecessarily ornate or pompous. A similar group of buildings can be found in Bauskas Street. The area does, however, have a few fancy buildings, too. At Ludviķa Street 2, for example, the building has an expressive little tower. It is here — between Ludviķa and Vēja streets — that a number of Art Nouveau single family homes are located. The building at Bauskas Street 16, for example, is a structure with towers and romantic balconies. The original details of the facade have been preserved to some extent, and the area above the bay is still "protected" by a realistically depicted dog. The dog's "brother" lives on the facade of the building at Šķūņu Street 10/12 in Old Rīga.

In 1911, Eižens Laube designed an apartment and shop building at Jelgavas Street 74, with two rusticated atlases on the entrance portal. Finally, we must mention the early 20th century apartment and shop building at Jelgavas Street 82. The oldest street in Pārdaugava — the twisting and hilly Vēja Street — begins at the building, and in its direction we see evidence of industrial Rīga from the earliest part of the 20th century. There are factory smokestacks and buildings which used to house people who, even in the period of Art Nouveau, thought more about everyday survival than they did about the latest trends in fashion. The presence of Art Nouveau in these buildings, however, can be found in the details — a wall blanket with swans and a statement of hope that someone would enjoy sweet dreams, for example, or a small vase from the Iļģuciems glass factory.

As we leave Pārdaugava, we have to pause at the apartment building at Kuģu Street 11/13, right on the shore of the Daugava River, by the stone bridge. It was put up in 1911 after a design by Eižens Laube and Augusts Malvess. Certain elements, such as the corner tower, remind us of several other Laube buildings, e.g. the Romanova Bazaar at Lāčplēša Street 70, 70a and 70b.

We should also remember that the Latvian Theater Museum is located in Eduarda Smiļģa Street in Pārdaugava. It contains exhibits that tell us about the history of the Latvian theater, in which Art Nouveau played a distinct role.

The **Torņakalna viaduct** (1908–1910, the "Weiss und Freitag" company) is one of the earliest examples of cement construction in Rīga and the entire Russian Empire. Elements of Art Nouveau are clearly seen in the bridge. The small street which runs alongside the railroad still contains buildings from the early 20th century, but the majestic and romantic mood of the area is enhanced by the Martin Luther Torņakalns Church (1888, architect Johannes Koch), behind which among trees there is the Torņakalns cemetery .

The building at Mazā Altonavas Street 6 (1903, architect Jānis Alksnis), which was originally used by the Latvian Aid Society, exposes certain principles of Historicism in its appearance. The design may be linked to the James Armitsted children's hospital which

Annas Sakses Street 5

CONCLUSION

This guide includes buildings that represent only a small part of the Art Nouveau heritage of Rīga. Also of importance in the city which flourished at the turn of the 19th and 20th centuries is the summer home region of Mežaparks, which was built up beginning in 1902. It is worth the effort to visit Mežaparks, where beautiful homes are nestled in serenity among pine trees. Many of the buildings in Sudrabu Edžus, Hamburgas, Sakses, Gdaņskas, Glika, Stokholmas, Hamburgas and Ščecinas streets were designed by the architects Gerhard von Tiesenhausen, Eduard Kupffer, Herman Seuberlich and other Baltic German architects.

Development of the garden city was connected with the tendencies to improve the living standards that were characteristic of the age. It was no accident that many buildings were improved in the early 20th century (in this connection we should remember the competition exhibition of 1907 "The Worker's House"), and the first complex blocks of buildings appeared in the urban environment. One example is so-called Forburg's block of buildings among Ausekļa, Sakaru and Eksporta streets, which were designed by Wilhelm Roman Roessler after a project competition in 1913. However, these buildings and their interiors, in line with the principles of Art Nouveau and the aesthetic criteria of the day, never really provided purely functional solutions. The beautiful and the practical was supposed to be in harmony, and that is one of the main reasons why anyone who walks around in Rīga inevitably finds the gaze drawn to buildings from the period of Art Nouveau.

Riga, 2000

Names of the building owners of the turn of the 19th and 20th century are occasionally preserved. The date of construction of buildings and information about the architects are based on data from the technical archives of the Rīga Main Architectural Board and on the publications of the architecture historian Jānis Krastiņš.

Bibliography

Berkholz, A. Moderne Rigasche Neubatten // Rigascher Almanach. — Rīga, 1903–1906.

Brancis, M. Jūgendstila izpausmes Rīgas 700 gadu jubilejas rūpniecības un amatniecības izstādē 1901. gadā (Manifestations of Art Nouveau in the 1901 industrial and trade exhibition that celebrated the 700th anniversary of Rīga) // Latvijas Zinātņu Akadēmijas Vēstis. — 1992. — No. 10. — pp. 37–43.

Caune, A. Rīgas vecpilsēta pirms 100 gadiem: Pilsēta un pilsētnieki 19. gs. beigu un 20. gs. sākuma atklātnēs (Rīga's old city 100 years ago: The city and its residents in postcards from the late 19th and early 20th century). — Rīga, 1994.

Caune, A. Rīgas Pārdaugava pirms 100 gadiem: Pārdaugavas iedzīvotāji 19. gs. beigu un 20. gs. sākuma atklātnēs (The Pārdaugava region of Rīga 100 years ago: The residents of Pārdaugava in postcards from the late 19th and early 20th century). — Rīga, 1998.

Dāvidsone, I. Rīgas dārzi un parki (Rīga's parks and gardens). — Rīga, 1988.

Grosa, S. Jūgendstila interjers Latvijā: Mākslu sintēzes un periodizācijas aspekti (Art Nouveau interiors in Latvia: Aspects of the synthesis and periods of the arts) // Latvijas Zinātņu Akadēmijas Vēstis. — 1998. — No. 1/2. — pp. 48–52.

Grosa, S. Trīs H. Šēla un F. Šefela interjeri Rīgas jūgendstila kontekstā (Three interiors by Heinrich Scheel and Friedrich Scheffel in the context of Rigensian Art Nouveau) // Materiāli par literatūru, folkloru, mākslu un arhitektūru (Materials about literature, folklore, art and architecture) / Sast./Ed. A. Rožkalne. — Rīga, 1999. — pp. 68–87.

Grosa, S. Vēlreiz par neoklasicismu Rīgas 19. un 20. gs. mijas dekoratīvajā tēlniecībā (Once more about Neo-Classicism in the decorative sculpture of Rīga at the turn of the 19th and 20th century) // Latvijas māksla starptautisko sakaru kontekstā: Rakstu krājums (Latvian art in the context of international contacts: Collection of papers) / Sast./Ed. S. Grosa. — Rīga, 2000.

Howard, J. Art Nouveau: International and National Styles in Europe. — Manchester: Manchester University Press, 1996.

Jūgendstils: Laiks un telpa: Baltijas jūras valstis 19.–20. gs. mijā (Art Nouveau: Time and space: The Baltic Sea countries at the turn of the 19th and 20th century) / Sast./Ed. S. Grosa. — Rīga, 1999.

Kļaviņš, E. Latvijas XIX gs. beigu un XX gs. sākuma tēlotājas mākslas ikonogrāfijā un stilistiskais raksturojums (Iconography and stylistic characteristics of the late 19th and early 20th century fine art). — Rīga, 1993.

Kļaviņš, E. Jūgendstils (Art Nouveau). — Rīga, 1994.

Krastiņš, J. Jūgendstils Rīgas arhitektūrā (Art Nouveau in the architecture of Rīga). — Rīga, 1980.

Krastiņš, J. Eklektisms Rīgas arhitektūrā (Eclecticism in the architecture of Rīga). — Rīga, 1988.

Krastiņš, J. Rīga — jūgendstila metropole (Rīga: An Art Nouveau metropolis). — Rīga, 1996.

Krastiņš, J. Mežaparks. — Rīga, 1997.

Lejnieks, J. Rīgas arhitektūra: Fotoalbums (Riga architecture: A photo album). — Rīga, 1989.

Rīga: 1860–1917. — Rīga, 1978.

Rozentāle (Grosa), S. Rīgas jūgendstila arhitektūras plastiskais rotājums (The plastic decorations of Art Nouveau architecture in Rīga) // Latviešu tēlotāja māksla. — Rīga, 1983. — pp. 109–127.

Schervinsky, M. Die Rigaer Jubileums Ausstellung 1901 in Bild und Wort. — Rīga, 1902.

www.jumava.lv

Publisher: SIA "Jumava", Dzirnavu Street 73, Riga LV 1011.
Printed by: Preses Nams Corp. "Jāņa sēta" Printing Group
Balasta dambis 3, Riga LV 1081.